TREASURE HUNT

Featuring

PRAYER PUPS

An Activity Book for Children
Ages 7-9

By Jeffrey Smith & Sebrina Zerkus Smith

BroadStreet
KIDS

Published by BroadStreet Kids
BroadStreet Kids is an imprint of

BroadStreet Publishing® Group, LLC
Savage, Minnesota, USA
BroadStreetPublishing.com

Treasure Hunt: Fun Activities and Devotions for Kids

Published in association with the literary agency, WTA Services LLC, Franklin, Tennessee

All Scripture quotations are from the Holy Bible, New Living Translation, copyright © 1996, 2004, 2007, 2013, 2015 by Tyndale House Foundation. Used by permission of Tyndale House Publishers, Inc., Carol Stream, Illinois 60188, USA. All rights reserved.

Stock or custom editions of BroadStreet Publishing titles may be purchased in bulk for educational, business, ministry, fundraising, or sales promotional use. For information, please email info@broadstreetpublishing.com.

Printed in the United States of America
18 19 20 21 22 5 4 3 2 1

To
Zane, Sarah, and Bekah

Thanks for inspiring the *Prayer Pups*!

Contents

Meet the Pups!

CON (CONSTANTINE)
A little pug with a lot of common sense. Con often helps the others find the truth of God's Word.

ABBY (ABIGAIL)
A poodle who loves looking pretty. God's always watching, so she wants to look her best.

NIM (NIMROD)
A chihuahua who usually speaks before he thinks, often resulting in ridiculous opinions.

AMOS
His desire for food is only outweighed by his love for God, but it's a really close call.

JERRY (JEREMIAH)
This dalmation thinks everyone should have spots. Jerry loves to tell really corny jokes.

D.T. (DOUBTIN' T)
Con's cousin from the city, D.T's not sure what to believe or where to find the answers.

Treasure #1

The Treasure of Today

PSALM 118:24

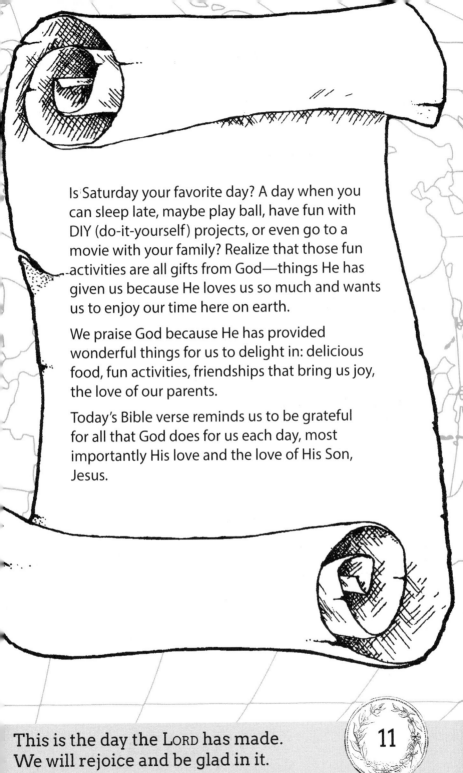

Is Saturday your favorite day? A day when you can sleep late, maybe play ball, have fun with DIY (do-it-yourself) projects, or even go to a movie with your family? Realize that those fun activities are all gifts from God—things He has given us because He loves us so much and wants us to enjoy our time here on earth.

We praise God because He has provided wonderful things for us to delight in: delicious food, fun activities, friendships that bring us joy, the love of our parents.

Today's Bible verse reminds us to be grateful for all that God does for us each day, most importantly His love and the love of His Son, Jesus.

This is the day the LORD has made.
We will rejoice and be glad in it.

Let's Begin Our Treasure Hunt!

First, pray to God and thank Him for all the wonderful things He has provided for you to enjoy. Whether today is rainy or sunny doesn't matter. What matters is that you are off on an important journey—to find God's hidden treasures. What a beautiful day for a Treasure Hunt!

Your first assignment is to match the numbers below to fill in the blanks with the proper letters.

A B C D E F G H I J K L M
17 3 19 7 14 5 4 23 24 10 26 22 15

N O P Q R S T U V W X Y Z
21 13 6 18 25 9 2 16 12 11 8 20 1

___ ___ ___ ___   ___ ___
2   23 24 9   24 9

___ ___ ___   ___ ___ ___
2   23 14   7   17 20

___ ___ ___   ___ ___ ___ ___
2   23 14   22 13 25 7

___ ___ ___   ___ ___ ___ ___
23 17 9   15 17 7   14

12

ISAIAH 45:3

Circle the Five Differences

I will give you treasures hidden
in the darkness—secret riches.

Treasure #2
The Treasure of Your Heart

MATTHEW 6:21

What do you think treasure is?

Do you think it's something movie pirates might find in an ancient cave like gold, silver, and jewels? Well, treasure is anything we value, such as a trophy or a new outfit, but it's also love, friendship, and fun times.

Matthew 6:21 makes clear that whatever we value will have our full attention. It is something we will protect and safeguard, think about and value. That's what's meant by "there your heart will also be."

While you may treasure things like a new toy or a blue ribbon, these things can tarnish over time. There's only one type of treasure that will never fade, break, or change in any way, and that is God's love and the love of His Son Jesus.

"Wherever your treasure is, there the desires of your heart will also be."

Dig Up These Words About Treasure

```
K K L B S X G S W F P R E C I O U S L S
Z P K O N M M X O P G C G O H H Y S E A
A C F R T V Y A N E C U D J K Y X M A P
G T R C U C Q X R U Y G M U G D Y W P P
N X I O N L H L J P Q X G K N M G Y R H
E T E J W E P C B I W H H X O X D E I I
C Y J Q I N E E H E U F R F V I I I M R
K K Q P P N A O K M V F Z X Q T A D J E
L S B O R S R H U O D T V Q X Q M Z Y K
A S R U P U L W E M E R A L D S O J E G
C N A O D B B W J Y W P K I E L N O S J
E B C V F L K A T T A P H U R L D H K S
O X E D O C J I X P K A V I H C J Q R D
T R L N S U Y C C V D L Q M D A B K O Z
W M E R P D U K M F Y A E K A K Z X R O
R V T U B W Q T K A P W K Y Z U Z L Y D
P S Y B T X Y T B R M E H N T C I M M F
E Q U Y V X I G R B H C L X C B A N J F
J Q A E Z H U S M M K J K G A T I N Y Z
B N G P R I N G K N D N N J E W E L Q Z
```

BRACELET	CROWN	DIAMOND
EMERALD	GEM	JEWEL
NECKLACE	PEARL	PRECIOUS
RING	RUBY	SAPPHIRE

16

DID YOU KNOW...

Amazing Heart Facts

Your heart is about the same size as your fist.

Your heart beats about 100,000 times per day and about 35 million times in a year. Over your lifetime, your heart will beat more than 2.5 billion times!

Squeeze a tennis ball and you're using about the same force your heart uses to pump blood out to the body.

Color What's Hidden in Your Heart

Your heart pumps about 2,000 gallons of blood every day!

Treasure #3

The Treasure of a Good Attitude

COLOSSIANS 3:12

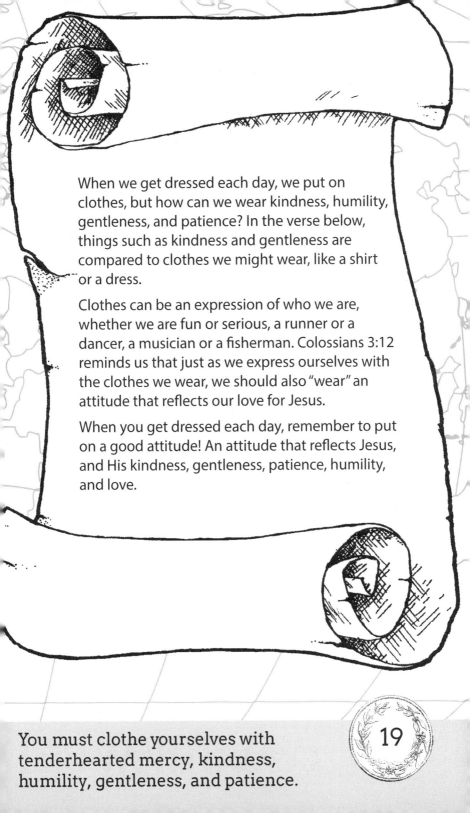

When we get dressed each day, we put on clothes, but how can we wear kindness, humility, gentleness, and patience? In the verse below, things such as kindness and gentleness are compared to clothes we might wear, like a shirt or a dress.

Clothes can be an expression of who we are, whether we are fun or serious, a runner or a dancer, a musician or a fisherman. Colossians 3:12 reminds us that just as we express ourselves with the clothes we wear, we should also "wear" an attitude that reflects our love for Jesus.

When you get dressed each day, remember to put on a good attitude! An attitude that reflects Jesus, and His kindness, gentleness, patience, humility, and love.

You must clothe yourselves with tenderhearted mercy, kindness, humility, gentleness, and patience.

Memorization Game

Memorize the verse on the previous page (Colossians 3:12), then write the things God wants you to clothe yourself in on the T-shirts below.

What Should Nim Wear?

Nim's just out of the shower and wants to get ready for church. List four things he should wear.

_____ SOCKS _____

_____

_____

_____

_____

Now, list 4 things he shouldn't wear.

_____ BLANKET _____

_____

_____

_____

_____

"Don't worry about these things, saying, 'What will we eat? What will we drink? What will we wear?'"

Treasure #4

The Treasure of Fellowship

FATHER, I DON'T KNOW HOW TO MAKE IT THROUGH THIS DIFFICULT TIME.

IT'S HARD TO DEAL WITH THE BURDENS THAT I'M FACING. BUT I KNOW YOU'RE WITH ME AND THAT YOU WILL ALWAYS GIVE ME WHAT I NEED TO CARRY ON.

LIKE ALL MY FRIENDS. THANK YOU FOR THEM.

22

COLOSSIANS 3:16

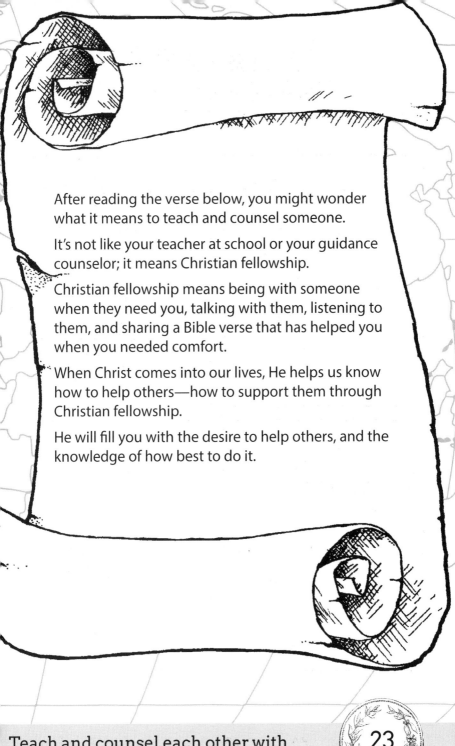

After reading the verse below, you might wonder what it means to teach and counsel someone.

It's not like your teacher at school or your guidance counselor; it means Christian fellowship.

Christian fellowship means being with someone when they need you, talking with them, listening to them, and sharing a Bible verse that has helped you when you needed comfort.

When Christ comes into our lives, He helps us know how to help others—how to support them through Christian fellowship.

He will fill you with the desire to help others, and the knowledge of how best to do it.

Teach and counsel each other with all the wisdom he gives.

Make Friends with This Word Search

```
W P U S C A J G U Q I T S S F S J Y V C
T A T N F K E Z I P I L Y I K P Q U Y T
I K K O D C T C A Q G Z M S D T K N A A
E T P F G E N W T M H T P T H C X I S M
P O F K D E R F Q F F X A E E P Z T K I
R D V U O F T S F R E T T R G D T Y E T
J N G R B I R H T O H K H H J R B I X Y
Z E G R A R K I E A W S Y O A D P P C Q
Q P M S R P C Z E R N V O O U G U J U L
B J E P O V Y I L N N D I D W K Z D C G
Z R Z S A K W Z M B D E I N E L X O B D
N I H H K T O J H C N S S N V S M V A I
Y D Z C S Y H P T H Z X H S G J E S S I
D L R M P R C Y O U R H R I G W G A C O
X N V P F U M G E R D E D S P J R C Y B
E Z E P L A E O Y C E S F Z U J L D S P
D T Y B P P W G A H C O O P E R A T E W
L M V R W E L A S X Q U F D K R T W Y H
J Q S D B C O M M U N I O N S L X L I N
M Q B R O T H E R H O O D B S S K S U L
```

AMITY	BROTHERHOOD	CHURCH
COMMUNION	COOPERATE	EMPATHY
FRIENDSHIP	SISTERHOOD	SYMPATHY
TOGETHERNESS	UNDERSTANDING	UNITY

24

IT'S A FACT...

Be a Good Friend

Make a list of all the ways you can help others.

_____

_____

_____

_____

Write the names of people who need your prayers.

_____

_____

_____

_____

25

Friendship is good for your health!

Treasure #5
The Treasure of Singing

PSALM 96:1

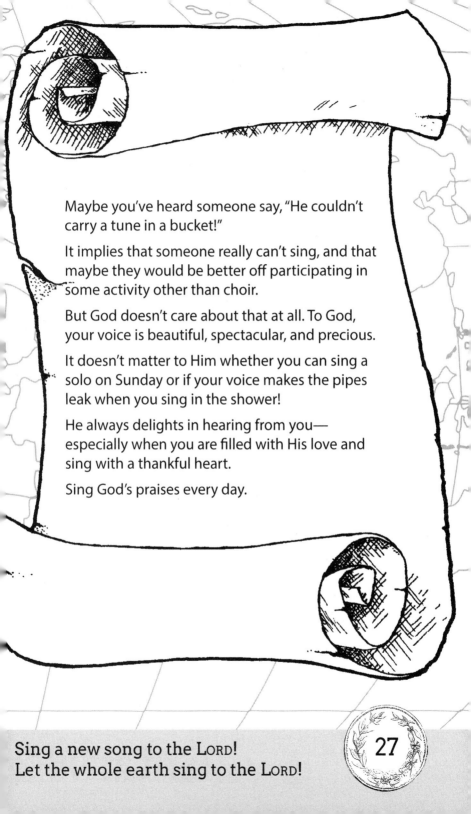

Maybe you've heard someone say, "He couldn't carry a tune in a bucket!"

It implies that someone really can't sing, and that maybe they would be better off participating in some activity other than choir.

But God doesn't care about that at all. To God, your voice is beautiful, spectacular, and precious.

It doesn't matter to Him whether you can sing a solo on Sunday or if your voice makes the pipes leak when you sing in the shower!

He always delights in hearing from you—especially when you are filled with His love and sing with a thankful heart.

Sing God's praises every day.

Sing a new song to the LORD!
Let the whole earth sing to the LORD!

Help Nim Get to Choir Practice on Time

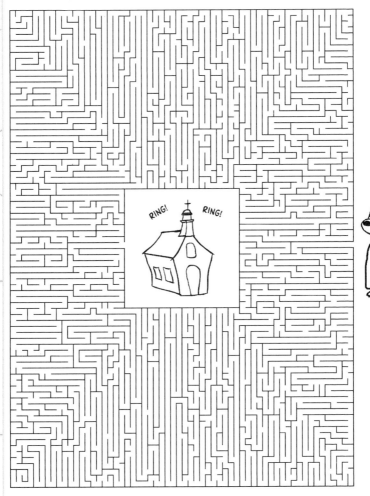

PSALM 96:2

Sing–Along Word Search

```
O K P O A Z Q R P D Z H Z O G K W O V J
O R X Q U H Y M N F J M P S M G K C K O
E M P Q E U H G G T U S X Y V O T K V Y
Y C R F W E P P J Z H K R X Z K K B T F
R H X W P S I O X V N M M A T X B V J U
P O D N X S D T B J F K X I B P Y O Y L
F I P W R H S N E B Q J O L G A D I A L
W R E L J O Y T C W E E T F B M O C B M
U L T S G U D P S A J S F K I E O E Q I
U F O O M T X M W G T U R W B U U Y O J
U P I B C H U R C H D S S V Y R S D M V
Y P R E A Y T N R F P B H M Q S Y W U P
I C R A H C Q F D A I X O K H N Q T Y D
D M J X I W B A G R V F P Q C H S Y Y M
W I G G G S M T G W F P J L O R D K M I
V B G R K T E E D G O E K N N E W F H Y
W O F D S S D D N E P N Q P J X L H O X
H L A T R Q E K R O Q N W O J M D N L Y
Q G S O N G S F P V Z S I N G N A Y Y P
B T E G J Q G A Z P J N E R U E Q B B J
```

CHOIR	CHURCH	HOLY
HYMN	JESUS	JOYFUL
LORD	PRAISE	SHOUT
SING	SONG	VOICE

Sing to the LORD; praise his name.
Each day proclaim the good news
that he saves.

29

Treasure #6

The Treasure of Representing Jesus

AMOS, I'M HIRING YOU AS MY STAND-IN.

STAND-IN? FOR WHAT?

THE BIBLE SAYS WE SHOULD DO EVERYTHING REPRESENTING JESUS.

THAT GOT ME THINKING ABOUT HAVING OTHERS REPRESENT ME WHILE I'M REPRESENTING JESUS. YOU'RE TALL, AND I THINK THAT REPRESENTS MY BEST REPRESENTATION OF WHO I WANT TO BE WHILE REPRESENTING JESUS.

THIS IS RIDICULOUS!

SILENCE, STAND-IN!!! THE STAR IS TALKING!

COLOSSIANS 3:17

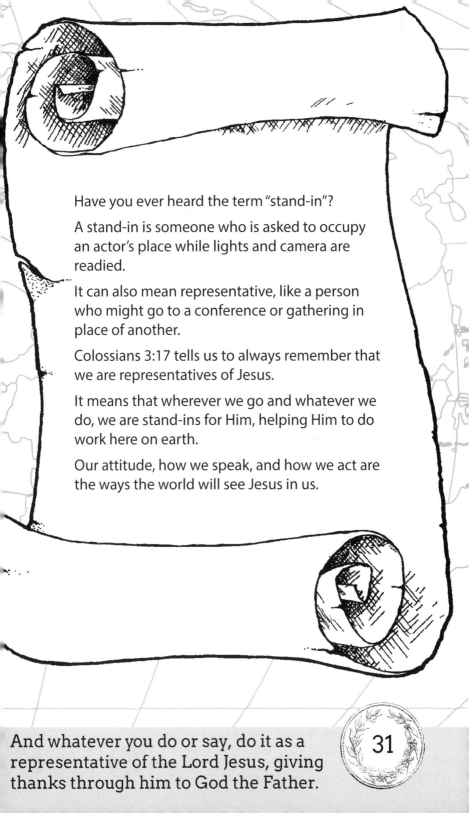

Have you ever heard the term "stand-in"?

A stand-in is someone who is asked to occupy an actor's place while lights and camera are readied.

It can also mean representative, like a person who might go to a conference or gathering in place of another.

Colossians 3:17 tells us to always remember that we are representatives of Jesus.

It means that wherever we go and whatever we do, we are stand-ins for Him, helping Him to do work here on earth.

Our attitude, how we speak, and how we act are the ways the world will see Jesus in us.

And whatever you do or say, do it as a representative of the Lord Jesus, giving thanks through him to God the Father.

Prayer Pups Superhero Movie

As the superhero "Prayer Warrior," Nim battles evil in his quest to represent Jesus! Color him.
- He stands for goodness!
- His prayers are faster than a speeding frisbee!
- He often gets tangled in his own cape!

BY DAY, AN ORDINARY PRAYER PUP. BY NIGHT, HE BECOMES THE...

Prayer Warrior

DO THIS:

Be a Good Stand-In

Make a list of the characteristics that make you a good representative of Jesus.

I am kind, and I like to share.

_____

_____

_____

_____

Color Nim the Director

Reading your Bible each day can help you understand how God wants you to represent Him.

Treasure #7
The Treasure of Wisdom

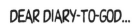

DEAR DIARY-TO-GOD...

I WAS READING COLOSSIANS 2:3 TODAY AND LEARNED THAT MY GREATEST TREASURE IS YOU.

I'VE ALWAYS TREASURED JEWELRY, CLOTHES AND OTHER PRETTY THINGS, BUT NOW I REALIZE THAT YOU'RE WHAT I TREASURE MOST. WHICH LEAVES ME WONDERING...

DO I NEED TO BUY A BIGGER JEWELRY BOX SO MY BIBLE WILL FIT INSIDE?

LOVE, ABBY

COLOSSIANS 2:3

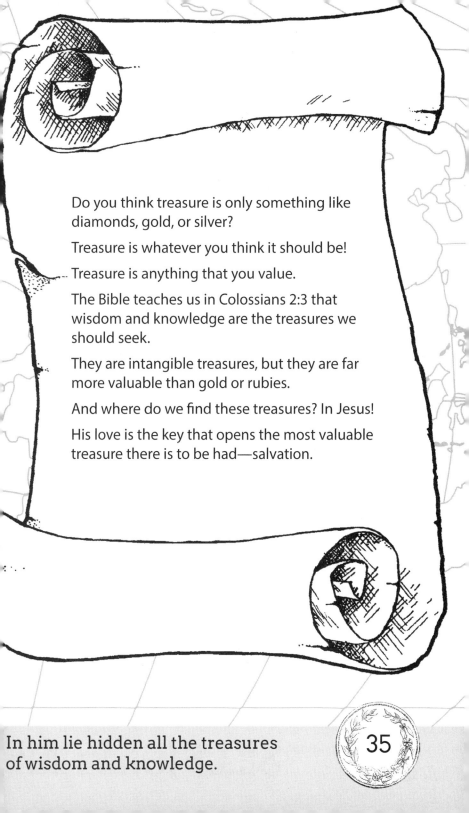

Do you think treasure is only something like diamonds, gold, or silver?

Treasure is whatever you think it should be!

Treasure is anything that you value.

The Bible teaches us in Colossians 2:3 that wisdom and knowledge are the treasures we should seek.

They are intangible treasures, but they are far more valuable than gold or rubies.

And where do we find these treasures? In Jesus!

His love is the key that opens the most valuable treasure there is to be had—salvation.

In him lie hidden all the treasures of wisdom and knowledge.

Nim Finds Wisdom (Sort of!)

Color Nim and Abby.

SILLY JOKE TIME

Are You Wise Enough for This Maze?

Con has lost his Bible. Can you help him find it?

What type of books do owls read?

Whooo-dunnits!

Treasure #8
The Treasure of Parables

CON'S BIG BIBLE FACTS

JESUS WOULD OFTEN TELL STORIES THAT WERE CALLED "PARABLES."

What is a Parable?

A parable is a story that teaches an important lesson by comparing one thing to something else.

Like saying "treasure" when talking about "God's love."

THE PARABLE OF THE FIELD IS LIKE THAT. WHEN THE MAN FINDS HIS TREASURE,

HE SELLS EVERYTHING HE HAS TO BUY IT.

That means once we discover our real treasure in Christ, we can't let anything else be more important.

38

MATTHEW 13:44

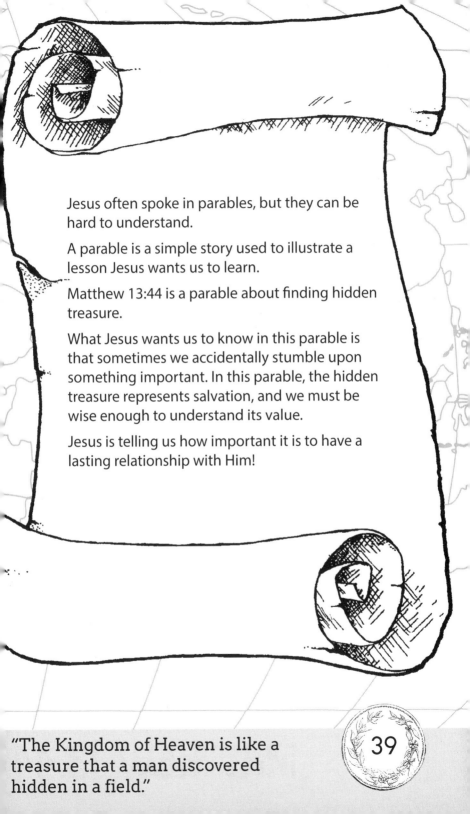

Jesus often spoke in parables, but they can be hard to understand.

A parable is a simple story used to illustrate a lesson Jesus wants us to learn.

Matthew 13:44 is a parable about finding hidden treasure.

What Jesus wants us to know in this parable is that sometimes we accidentally stumble upon something important. In this parable, the hidden treasure represents salvation, and we must be wise enough to understand its value.

Jesus is telling us how important it is to have a lasting relationship with Him!

"The Kingdom of Heaven is like a treasure that a man discovered hidden in a field."

Hidden Words Word Search

```
B U V C S B B R V F K V D D S G W Z F K
C Q I H W O O U V E H Q Y S M P J K S U
C W Z U V Y L C R P R T W P Y K J D U N
Z O V G Z I J L M I S Z B C S J P F B S
G Q V Z C H R O W L E T Z Y T M M N A E
E E I E O V S A Q J U D K L I J M Z S E
J A Q E R V F K N I O K M R C Q W Z H N
K R P L B E Z E Q B L N B V A N W P R S
G V G F G M D D S Q L B G B L S I U O F
F G J V M B T K P X P Q D T K G Z N U C
Y C P U V Q W M W G K N L L F B M L D I
J Z L M Y S T E R I O U S R T O D H E N
I T Z O M D I S G U I S E D H P X J D V
Q P D J U O Q D H T B A W S Z W Q S G I
Z N L S Z D B A K R A W O H R B B O A S
R C V N T V E W B T T R F K D D I Q L I
U N V K D U A D Z K Y W Q P A F F F Z B
D F O P T H X Z T K T E Z E E Q P X Z L
H O C O N C E A L E D E J D J C P S C E
B P X D V E I L E D Q J C I A F O C S A
```

BURIED   CLOAKED   CLOUDED

CONCEALED   COVERED   DISGUISED

INVISIBLE   MYSTERIOUS   MYSTICAL

SHROUDED   UNSEEN   VEILED

MATTHEW 13:44

Secret Code—Can You Decipher It?

How did the dolphin trainer answer God's call?

1=H 2=R 3=O 4=N 5=L 6=U 7=A 8=E 9=P
10=C 11=Y 12=B 13=S 14=I 15=M 16=G

```
 __ __     __ __ __ __ __     __ __ __
 12 11      6 13 14  4 16      1 14 13

__ __ __ __ __ __ __     __ __ __ __ __ __ __ __ !
13  9  8 10 14  7  5      9  3  2  9  3 14 13  8
```

Hide & Seek Maze

READY OR NOT,
HERE I COME!

"In his excitement, he hid it again and sold everything he owned to get enough money to buy the field."

Treasure #9

The Treasure of Baptism

42

MATTHEW 3:16

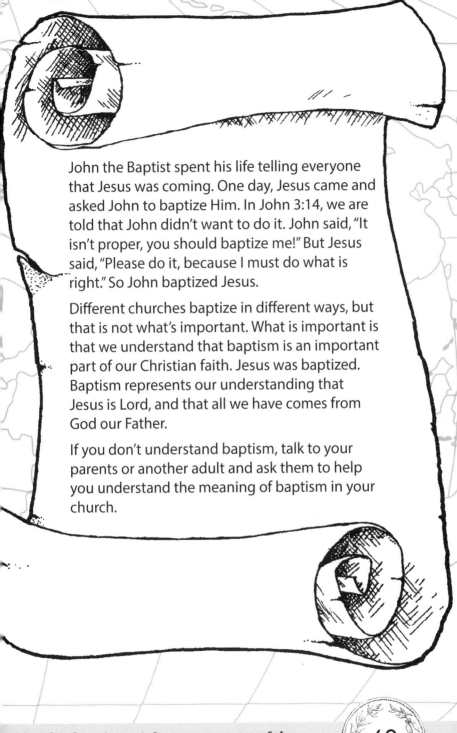

John the Baptist spent his life telling everyone that Jesus was coming. One day, Jesus came and asked John to baptize Him. In John 3:14, we are told that John didn't want to do it. John said, "It isn't proper, you should baptize me!" But Jesus said, "Please do it, because I must do what is right." So John baptized Jesus.

Different churches baptize in different ways, but that is not what's important. What is important is that we understand that baptism is an important part of our Christian faith. Jesus was baptized. Baptism represents our understanding that Jesus is Lord, and that all we have comes from God our Father.

If you don't understand baptism, talk to your parents or another adult and ask them to help you understand the meaning of baptism in your church.

After his baptism, as Jesus came out of the water, the heavens opened and he saw the Spirit of God descending like a dove and settling on him.

From Nim's Bad Idea Files: High Dive Baptisms

THE PREACHER PUSHES PEOPLE INTO THE WATER FROM THE HIGHEST-DIVE AT A SWIMMING POOL! THEY GET TO ACCEPT JESUS AND CONQUER THEIR FEAR OF HEIGHTS AT THE SAME TIME!

H²O

YOU'RE SAVED!

AAAA!

Now That's a Bad Idea!

44

Word Search Splash

```
B E C R G B F Z J C P Z Y S F
Z G R D B E S R F B F E E C Q
A H O I D K F T U G R H A Z E
Q G U F X L A O V I T D R B S
V Q G P B E R E O A T B B K T
R L H H H C O V R D S O P Z O
D P A W M F O W U T F Q I A N
I U G Q O Y T L X X Q Y I X E
L C A C U T M P W B R C W P S
B H D X N K W N Q T M N H R V
A A F P T T B I N O E E O D E V
P F J A A K X U S H A R E A U
T F S B I T O R C C F R D C S
I O E X N C R Y U E K F E H F
S X J T B B T E R R J A T I L
M D Y J I J Y I E P P A N N E
J G I T U E F I B S P B S G E
Z Q K E T E B G Z Y S J O G A
```

AX	BAPTISM	CHAFF	COUNTRY	CUT
FIRE	FLEE	FOOD	FRUIT	MOUNTAIN
PATHS	PREACHING	ROOT	ROUGH	SHARE
STONES	TREES	WHEAT	WRATH	YEAR

45

And a voice from heaven said,
"This is my dearly loved Son,
who brings me great joy."

Treasure #10

PROVERBS 18:10

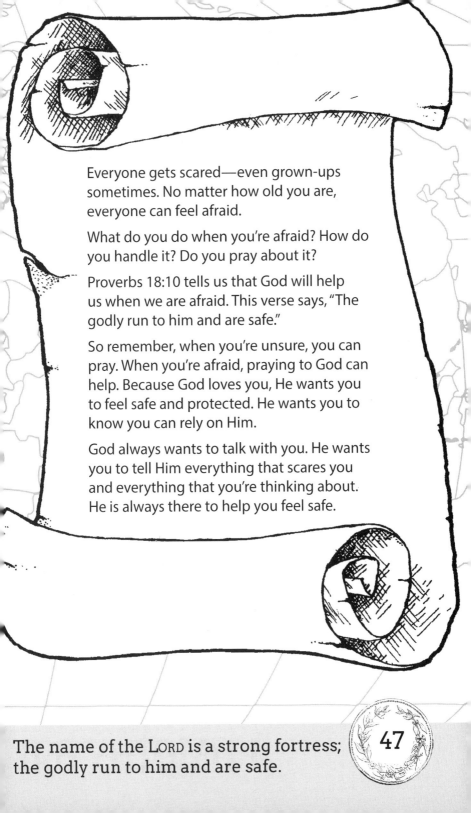

Everyone gets scared—even grown-ups sometimes. No matter how old you are, everyone can feel afraid.

What do you do when you're afraid? How do you handle it? Do you pray about it?

Proverbs 18:10 tells us that God will help us when we are afraid. This verse says, "The godly run to him and are safe."

So remember, when you're unsure, you can pray. When you're afraid, praying to God can help. Because God loves you, He wants you to feel safe and protected. He wants you to know you can rely on Him.

God always wants to talk with you. He wants you to tell Him everything that scares you and everything that you're thinking about. He is always there to help you feel safe.

The name of the LORD is a strong fortress;
the godly run to him and are safe.

Help Jerry Find Help

Draw a line to connect Jerry to the people or things that can help him feel safe.

Police Officer

Banana

Firefighter

Notebook

Fire Extinguisher

Pastor

Bicycle

Parent

Friend

Stranger

1 TIMOTHY 6:11

How to Stay Safe Online

The Internet can be a fun place and a great way to chat, share photos, and listen to music.

BUT BE SMART TO STAY SAFE!

Abby's 5 Rules to Stay Safe Online!

Don't talk to anyone online
your parents don't know.

Don't send anyone pictures of yourself or
your family. Get a parent's help with this.

Always remember that you can block
anyone you want from messaging you.

Keep your phone number
and email address safe and secure.

If you find anything online that makes you
uncomfortable, tell your parents right away!

 STAYING SAFE ONLINE IS COOL.
TALK TO YOUR PARENTS TO
FIND MORE IDEAS!

Pursue righteousness and a godly life,
along with faith, love, perseverance,
and gentleness.

Treasure #11

The Treasure of Understanding

I'VE BEEN READING PROVERBS.

THAT'S GREAT. IT'S A REALLY GOOD BOOK.

WE CAN ALL GET A LOT OF REAL WISDOM FROM READING THE BOOK OF PROVERBS.

I KNOW.

YOU KNOW, A BUNCH OF PEOPLE THINK THAT I'M VERY WISE.

THEY DO?

OH YEAH, THEY DON'T EVER SAY IT, BUT I CAN TELL THEY'RE THINKING IT!

50

PROVERBS 2:3–4

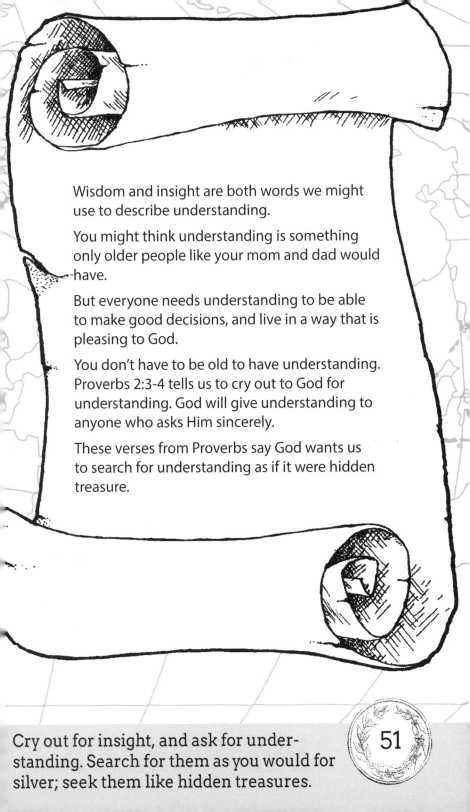

Wisdom and insight are both words we might use to describe understanding.

You might think understanding is something only older people like your mom and dad would have.

But everyone needs understanding to be able to make good decisions, and live in a way that is pleasing to God.

You don't have to be old to have understanding. Proverbs 2:3-4 tells us to cry out to God for understanding. God will give understanding to anyone who asks Him sincerely.

These verses from Proverbs say God wants us to search for understanding as if it were hidden treasure.

Cry out for insight, and ask for under-standing. Search for them as you would for silver; seek them like hidden treasures.

Help Professor Amos Solve This Puzzle

Use the words below to fill in the blanks. Write each boxed letter into the big boxes at the bottom to learn what God gave to Professor Amos.

KNOWLEDGE   INSIGHT   SILVER
UNDERSTANDING   PROVERBS   MAPS

_ _ _ ☐ _ _ _ _ _

☐ _ _ _ _ _

☐ _ _ _ _ _

_ _ ☐ _ _ _ _ _ _ _ _ _ _

_ _ ☐ _ _ _ _ _

☐ _ _ _

☐ ☐ ☐ ☐ ☐ ☐

52

DID YOU KNOW...

Color Amos

Proverbs are biblical sayings used
to state a general truth or give advice.

Treasure #12

The Treasure of Church

ARE YOU READY FOR CHURCH?

I'M NOT GOING.

I'VE READ THE WHOLE BIBLE. COVER TO COVER! NOW I HAVE NOTHING TO LEARN THERE.

WELL, LUKE 4:16 SAYS THAT EVEN JESUS HIMSELF WENT TO CHURCH. AND HE'S THE SON OF GOD!

UM...WELL...I GUESS "MAYBE" THERE'S A LITTLE I COULD STILL LEARN.

54

LUKE 4:16

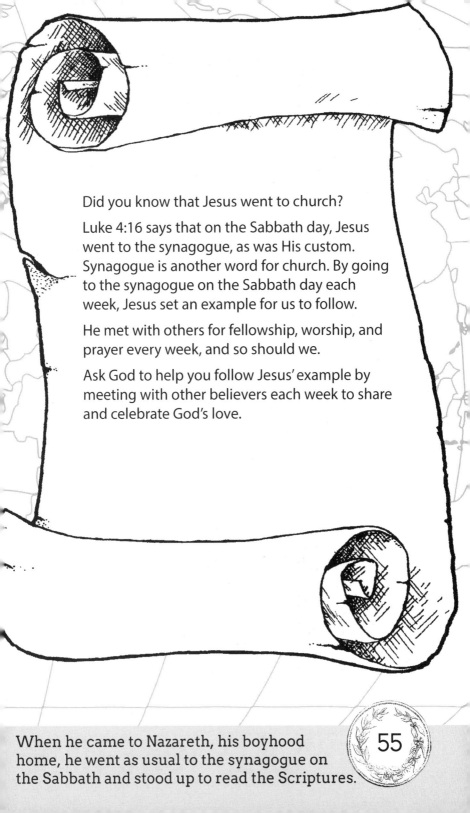

Did you know that Jesus went to church?

Luke 4:16 says that on the Sabbath day, Jesus went to the synagogue, as was His custom. Synagogue is another word for church. By going to the synagogue on the Sabbath day each week, Jesus set an example for us to follow.

He met with others for fellowship, worship, and prayer every week, and so should we.

Ask God to help you follow Jesus' example by meeting with other believers each week to share and celebrate God's love.

When he came to Nazareth, his boyhood home, he went as usual to the synagogue on the Sabbath and stood up to read the Scriptures.

List Things Con & Amos Do in Church

Pray

_____   _____

_____   _____

_____   _____

SILLY JOKE TIME:

Fill It In!

COLOR THE BOXES WITH 0'S ONE COLOR.
COLOR THE BOXES WITH 1'S ANOTHER COLOR.
WATCH WHAT APPEARS IN THE MIDDLE!

0	0	0	0	0	0	0	0
0	0	0	1	1	0	0	0
0	0	0	1	1	0	0	0
0	1	1	1	1	1	1	0
0	1	1	1	1	1	1	0
0	0	0	1	1	0	0	0
0	0	0	1	1	0	0	0
0	0	0	1	1	0	0	0
0	0	0	1	1	0	0	0
0	0	0	0	0	0	0	0

Why can't Prayer Pups dance?
Because they have two left feet!

Treasure #13

The Treasure of New Life

SO A CATERPILLAR SPINS A COCOON AROUND ITSELF.

THEN LATER, IT EMERGES FROM THAT DISGUSTING, STINKY CHRYSALIS AS AN AWESOME NEW CREATION...A BEAUTIFUL, COLORFUL BUTTERFLY.

THAT'S A LOT LIKE OUR REBIRTH INTO NEW LIFE BY GOD'S SAVING GRACE.

BUT A LOT MORE GROSS!

OH YEAH, ABSOLUTELY!

58

1 PETER 1:23

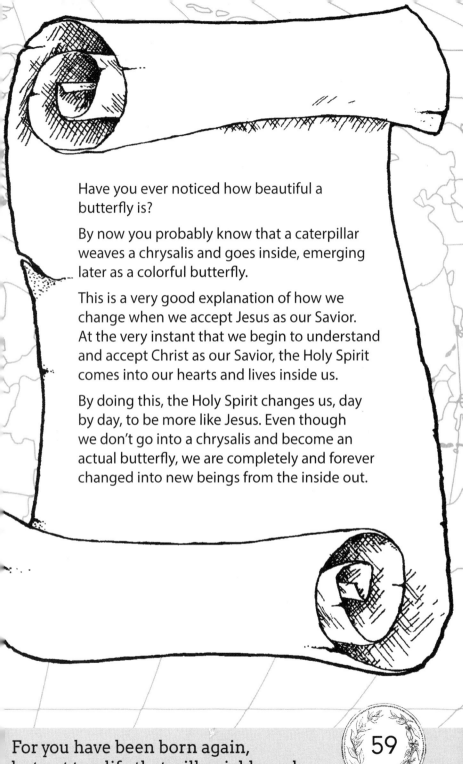

Have you ever noticed how beautiful a butterfly is?

By now you probably know that a caterpillar weaves a chrysalis and goes inside, emerging later as a colorful butterfly.

This is a very good explanation of how we change when we accept Jesus as our Savior. At the very instant that we begin to understand and accept Christ as our Savior, the Holy Spirit comes into our hearts and lives inside us.

By doing this, the Holy Spirit changes us, day by day, to be more like Jesus. Even though we don't go into a chrysalis and become an actual butterfly, we are completely and forever changed into new beings from the inside out.

For you have been born again,
but not to a life that will quickly end.

Did You Know...

The monarch butterfly is probably the best known butterfly in North America although it is found in other places around the world. It is known for its distinctive orange and black pattern. Its wingspan can reach 5 inches! These beautiful and prized  butterflies migrate north in the spring and south in the cooler months. The females lay their eggs during the long migration period. Monarch butterflies are one of the few insects that are capable of making a transatlantic crossing. That is why they've turned up in places like Bermuda, and as far away as Australia. Butterflies do not start out as butterflies. A butterfly larva grows to become a caterpillar, then spins a silk pad, which is attached to a leaf or twig, and forms a cocoon. As the caterpillar inside the cocoon matures, it grows to become a butterfly. After about two weeks inside the cocoon, the monarch butterfly emerges and flies away to feed on flowers such as milkweed, red clover, and goldenrod.

A-nutter Butterfly Joke?

Why couldn't the butterfly come to the dance?
Because it was a Moth Ball!

What do butterflies learn in school?
Mothmatics!

1 PETER 1:23

Flyaway Butterfly Word Search

```
Z I K O A V M G L N B F O V B
K O U N N I U X I I M A C Z L
Q Q D P O T T J W I D V Q T H
W O S Y I L E L N G C O M P E
I B O G N E S D F O W R H K A
T Y C L T K T Z E L C I A I L
N N H V E H I C T Z L T N P I
E G O M D S F O R B F I G R N
S K S L P E Y U E E N S I E G
S A E A W H E N E E I M N A T
E A N R V G X T I J A L G C Y
S M R O A S X R G D I T P H V
H C G S P K D Y W V N I R E A
U K S E K A U A E T E E J D N
S E Y E K F G L Z H W W Y X J
M H A C C E P T S O R I E T Z
J E S U S E P Z P O G N W B L
```

FAVORITISM	ACCEPTS	MESSAGE	PREACHED	ANOINTED
JESUS	POWER	HEALING	TESTIFY	WITNESSES
COUNTRY	HANGING	TREE	CHOSEN	AROSE

Your new life will last forever because it comes from the eternal, living word of God.

Treasure #14

The Treasure of God's Strength

 I'M A LITTLE CLAY JAR, SHORT AND STOUT.

 SAVED BY GRACE WITHOUT A DOUBT.

WHEN I GO TO CHURCH, YOU CAN HEAR ME SHOUT...

I'M LOVED BY GOD FROM THE INSIDE OUT!

2 CORINTHIANS 4:7

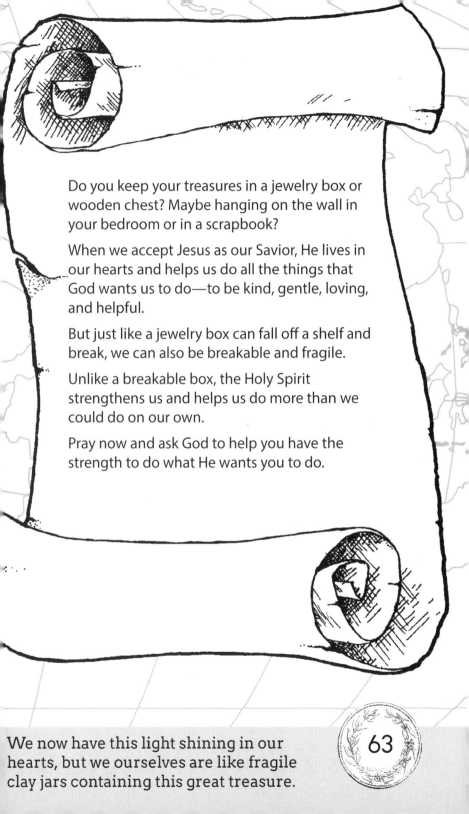

Do you keep your treasures in a jewelry box or wooden chest? Maybe hanging on the wall in your bedroom or in a scrapbook?

When we accept Jesus as our Savior, He lives in our hearts and helps us do all the things that God wants us to do—to be kind, gentle, loving, and helpful.

But just like a jewelry box can fall off a shelf and break, we can also be breakable and fragile.

Unlike a breakable box, the Holy Spirit strengthens us and helps us do more than we could do on our own.

Pray now and ask God to help you have the strength to do what He wants you to do.

We now have this light shining in our hearts, but we ourselves are like fragile clay jars containing this great treasure.

Strength through Prayer

What Do You Pray About?

_____   _____

_____   _____

2 CORINTHIANS 4:7

Weak vs. Strong Listing Game

On the left, list things that are strong; on the right, list things that are weak.

Strong	Weak
Steel	Noodles
Diamonds	Paper

This makes it clear that our great power is from God, not from ourselves.

Treasure #15

The Treasure of Prayer

"SOMETIMES I LIKE TO SING GOD'S PRAISES WITH ALL MY FRIENDS AT A CONCERT."

"SOMETIMES I LIKE TO STUDY THE WORD OF GOD IN A SMALL GROUP SETTING."

"BUT SOMETIMES I JUST LIKE TO SPEND QUALITY TIME ALONE WITH GOD. JUST ME AND HIM."

"THAT'S THE TIME I LIKE BEST OF ALL!"

MATTHEW 26:36

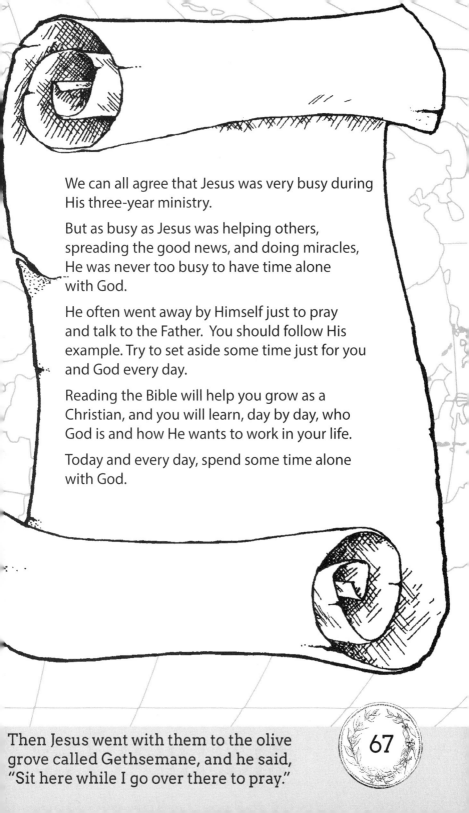

We can all agree that Jesus was very busy during His three-year ministry.

But as busy as Jesus was helping others, spreading the good news, and doing miracles, He was never too busy to have time alone with God.

He often went away by Himself just to pray and talk to the Father. You should follow His example. Try to set aside some time just for you and God every day.

Reading the Bible will help you grow as a Christian, and you will learn, day by day, who God is and how He wants to work in your life.

Today and every day, spend some time alone with God.

Then Jesus went with them to the olive grove called Gethsemane, and he said, "Sit here while I go over there to pray."

Prayer Is Important Word Search

```
S H P N E O N Q K H F X P A M J I C W T
H F S B Q E R V J G X I P V S G J S Z S
C E N S R I B Z X T L V W E V K G I N X
I C A U S P J R U P D O R D R I H E S S
X V R V Q F Z L V F E V B Z S M N H I T
W Z G U E Z F F E K V H E Q B I B L E A
D V W W I N S V J U O Q T I M E Y S W P
W C A L L I A V Q V T N E N X F S Q C P
H O D C T H Y M W U I D K X M T X W X E
R C R K O M Q J G D O N I W T A L Z B A
T Z O D A M I F C E N P G U O H O E I L
B Q V G U X M S N B H C T F R I L J T C
S R Q K N R A U F Z V O I M U B E E G G
M R L R X A A K N D D T L V X V F S B V
V V T V G I V E N I G D Q Y I E O U Z H
I F T S E R V I C E O M K U F A O S M W
U G E G M Y J E Y V T N M F M J V I D S
I P L E A M S Y F K S T V H D M O D Y L
W O R S H I P T E P F A T H E R D X I M
K Z R O V S B D L F Y A I Q B M Q I X B
```

APPEAL	ASK	BIBLE
COMMUNION	DEVOTION	FATHER
GIVEN	HEAVEN	HOLY
JESUS	PLEA	SERVICE
TIME	WORD	WORSHIP

68

MATTHEW 14:23

Draw Different Expressions on Nim

Nim loves to pray and spend time alone with God. What emotions do you think Nim feels as he prays? Draw them!

After sending them home, he went up into the hills by himself to pray. Night fell while he was there alone.

Treasure #16
The Treasure of Our Forever Home

2 CORINTHIANS 5:1

Do you know how to find your way home?

Did you know that heaven is also your home?

Heaven is your eternal home. A home where you can be with Jesus forever.

Jesus has left us clear directions to find our eternal home with him. Follow Jesus. He is "the way, the truth and the life" (John 14:6).

He is the way because through Jesus, we know the Father (God). He is the truth because Jesus is all of God's promises made real. He is the life because He joins His life to ours when we believe in Him.

Ask Jesus now to help you hear His voice, and follow Him home.

We will have a house in heaven, an eternal body made for us by God himself.

This Is Jerry's Home

Draw Your Home Below

DID YOU KNOW...

Help Jerry Find His Way Home

Heaven is a city. The apostle John saw "the holy city, the new Jerusalem" (Revelation 21:2).

Treasure #17

The Treasure of Gratitude

WHAT DO YOU VIEW AS THE WORLD'S BIGGEST PROBLEM?

THAT'S EASY...LACK OF GRATITUDE.

IF WE WERE ALL JUST MORE GRATEFUL FOR WHAT GOD HAS GIVEN US INSTEAD OF WORRYING ABOUT WHAT WE DON'T HAVE, MOST OF THE WORLD'S PROBLEMS WOULD BE CLEARED UP. WHAT DO YOU THINK IS THE BIGGEST PROBLEM TODAY?

LACK OF COOKIES.

74

PSALM 138:1

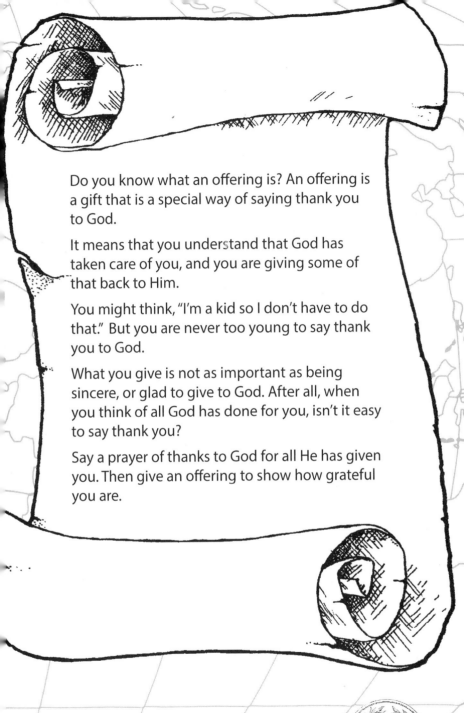

Do you know what an offering is? An offering is a gift that is a special way of saying thank you to God.

It means that you understand that God has taken care of you, and you are giving some of that back to Him.

You might think, "I'm a kid so I don't have to do that." But you are never too young to say thank you to God.

What you give is not as important as being sincere, or glad to give to God. After all, when you think of all God has done for you, isn't it easy to say thank you?

Say a prayer of thanks to God for all He has given you. Then give an offering to show how grateful you are.

I give you thanks, O Lord, with all my heart; I will sing your praises.

Grateful for Another Word Search

```
U  J  A  Z  M  O  I  N  T  R  H  V  C  R  R  E  Q  S  T  A
D  E  C  P  U  F  N  V  X  C  O  S  M  Y  E  D  T  A  H  Z
Q  A  S  T  P  H  J  M  R  A  I  B  S  F  C  B  D  G  A  R
I  D  K  I  X  R  G  C  W  O  D  Y  F  O  O  R  M  A  N  J
K  V  V  O  H  D  E  B  T  W  C  U  E  D  G  P  F  S  K  T
E  T  W  T  D  V  L  C  Y  R  B  R  J  H  N  G  G  P  S  B
O  P  O  M  P  C  E  G  I  V  W  X  B  X  I  R  R  N  G  S
X  B  C  B  N  V  S  D  V  A  O  V  V  T  T  A  A  O  I  S
C  V  L  O  P  D  O  R  K  E  T  O  W  X  I  T  C  T  V  N
W  W  W  I  Z  S  Z  K  C  C  Z  E  H  H  O  I  E  E  I  F
Z  W  A  I  G  P  A  U  N  K  T  Q  B  H  N  T  E  C  N  U
A  V  W  E  H  E  T  H  A  N  K  F  U  L  D  U  W  Z  G  W
K  A  P  Q  J  A  S  K  C  G  I  P  O  T  X  D  R  T  H  D
F  K  Y  C  G  B  I  D  N  U  J  R  G  P  K  E  I  E  O  E
W  A  L  X  L  Y  C  H  O  J  R  A  D  R  D  I  C  U  N  X
C  V  U  H  C  D  V  N  T  S  G  I  A  T  P  J  G  G  O  F
E  A  G  Z  V  W  U  D  I  Y  O  S  S  B  P  D  G  U  R  J
J  O  B  L  I  G  A  T  I  O  N  E  T  Z  D  K  R  Z  P  M
V  Y  M  Z  H  T  O  C  Z  P  D  V  A  S  X  Z  S  M  B  F
H  E  Z  S  X  B  U  F  O  G  R  A  T  E  F  U  L  C  B  D
```

APPRECIATE	DEBT	GRACE
GRATEFUL	GRATITUDE	HONOR
OBLIGATION	OBLIGE	PRAISE
RECOGNITION	THANKFUL	THANKSGIVING

76

THANK YOU!

DIY: Start a Family Gratitude Box

What You'll Need:

old shoebox	Bible	construction paper
wrapping paper	scissors	stickers & markers
pencil or pen	notepad	tape & glue

First, use the scissors to cut a small hole or slit into the top of the shoebox. Next, decorate the shoebox any way you want! You might cover it with wrapping paper or construction paper and write "Gratitude Box" on the side with markers, or cover the shoebox with stickers that remind you of being grateful. Or, use your Bible to find verses about being grateful and write those on the outside of your box. It's up to you!

After you have decorated your Gratitude Box, place it where everyone will see it and remember it, like in the family room or kitchen. Place the notepad and pencil next to the box.

Each time you or a family member walks by the box, write something for which you are grateful and add it to the box. For example, "My brother helped me clean my room," or "I'm glad I got to go swimming." At the end of a few weeks, open the box and read the notes together!

Gratitude Scavenger Hunt

Look at the list below, and for each line collect something for which you are grateful. Ask a friend to join you! Put an X by each item as you find it.

- ☐ Something that has words on it.
- ☐ Something that is colorful.
- ☐ Something that is older than you are.
- ☐ Something that smells goods.
- ☐ Something that makes you feel strong.
- ☐ Something that makes you laugh.
- ☐ Something that tastes good.
- ☐ Something that makes a beautiful sound.
- ☐ Something from nature.

At least once a day, make sure that you say "Thank you!" to God.

77

Treasure #18

The Treasure of God's Love

MY PASTOR SAID GOD IS LOVE.

THAT'S RIGHT.

BUT THE WORD LOVE IS A VERB, LIKE IN "I LOVE TO DANCE." SAYING SOMEONE IS A VERB DOESN'T MAKE SENSE. MAYBE I SHOULD START SAYING, "ABBY _IS_ DANCE."

LOVE CAN ALSO BE A NOUN, LIKE IN "HE HAS A LOT OF LOVE." IT'S USED LIKE THAT.

OH.

CAN I STILL SAY "ABBY IS DANCE?"

EPHESIANS 3:18

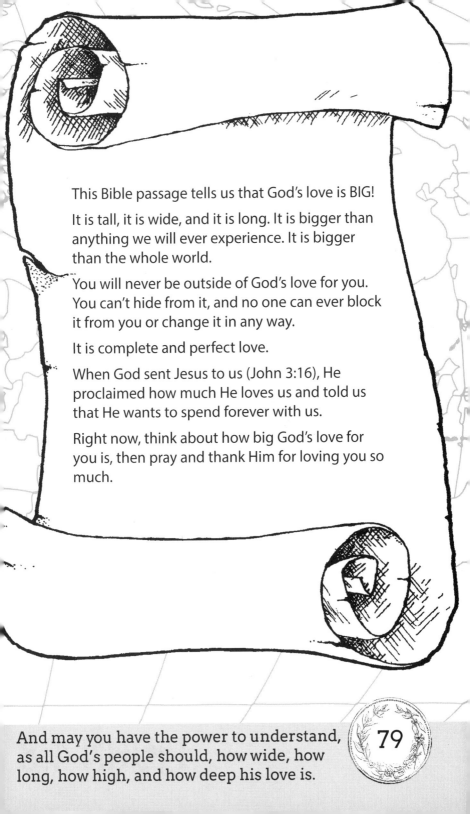

This Bible passage tells us that God's love is BIG!

It is tall, it is wide, and it is long. It is bigger than anything we will ever experience. It is bigger than the whole world.

You will never be outside of God's love for you. You can't hide from it, and no one can ever block it from you or change it in any way.

It is complete and perfect love.

When God sent Jesus to us (John 3:16), He proclaimed how much He loves us and told us that He wants to spend forever with us.

Right now, think about how big God's love for you is, then pray and thank Him for loving you so much.

And may you have the power to understand, as all God's people should, how wide, how long, how high, and how deep his love is.

Color the Pups

Always Remember...

GOD LOVES YOU!

What's the easiest way to get to heaven?

1=H 2=D 3=T 4=N 5=A 6=U 7=R 8=I 9=G
10=C 11=S 12=Y 13=O 14=K 15=L 16=M

$\overline{3}$ $\overline{6}$ $\overline{7}$ $\overline{4}$ $\quad$ $\overline{7}$ $\overline{8}$ $\overline{9}$ $\overline{1}$ $\overline{3}$ $\quad$ $\overline{5}$ $\overline{4}$ $\overline{2}$

$\overline{9}$ $\overline{13}$ $\quad$ $\overline{11}$ $\overline{3}$ $\overline{7}$ $\overline{5}$ $\overline{8}$ $\overline{9}$ $\overline{1}$ $\overline{3}$!

80

1 JOHN 4:8

Now Draw Something You Love

Another Funny Joke

What did one blueberry say to the other blueberry?

I love you berry much!

But anyone who does not love does not know God, for God is love.

Treasure #19

The Treasure of God's Word

YO! ABBY, WORD TO YOUR MOTHER!

HUH?

THE BIBLE IS CALLED "THE WORD." SO I'M SPREADING THE "WORD," BUT LIKE A RAPPER.

THAT'S GREAT, BUT YOU DON'T HAVE TO BE A RAPPER TO SPREAD THE WORD.

TRUE DAT. BUT THIS MAKES IT OFF THE CHAIN. YASSSSS!

YOU ARE SO ODD.

WORD, YO!

82

JOHN 17:17

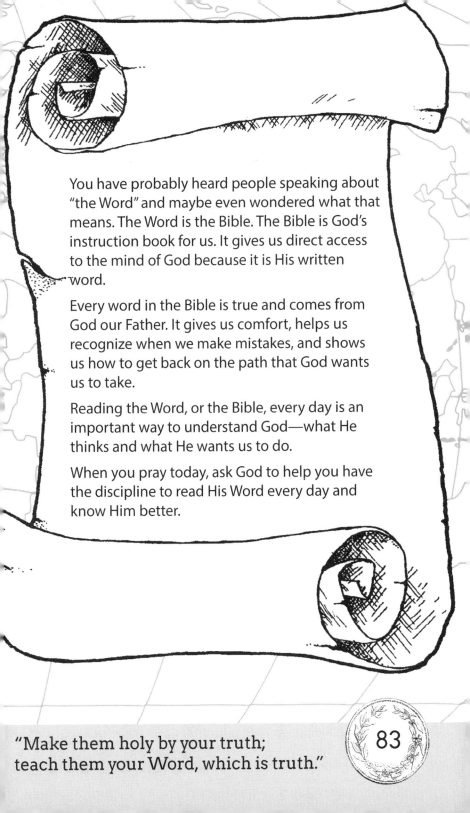

You have probably heard people speaking about "the Word" and maybe even wondered what that means. The Word is the Bible. The Bible is God's instruction book for us. It gives us direct access to the mind of God because it is His written word.

Every word in the Bible is true and comes from God our Father. It gives us comfort, helps us recognize when we make mistakes, and shows us how to get back on the path that God wants us to take.

Reading the Word, or the Bible, every day is an important way to understand God—what He thinks and what He wants us to do.

When you pray today, ask God to help you have the discipline to read His Word every day and know Him better.

"Make them holy by your truth; teach them your Word, which is truth."

Finding the Right Word

CON WANTS TO TELL D.T. ABOUT JESUS.
CIRCLE THE WORDS HE SHOULD USE:

LOVE	HAPPY	CARING	KITE
HOLY	MOUSE	SMART	LIFE

THEN COLOR THE PICTURE!

COOL FACT:

Find a Hidden Word DIY Project

What You'll Need:

white paper
white crayon
another crayon, color of your choice
tape or glue
watercolor palette
small cup for water
small brush

Here's How:

Using the white crayon, write or draw your message onto the white paper. Press firmly, but not so firmly that the letters show on the paper. Fold the paper and seal using tape or glue. Use the other crayon to address the message to your friend, or to draw your personal seal on the outside. Instruct your friend to open the sealed letter, then dip the small brush into the water and choose a color from the watercolor palette. Paint the watercolor all over the white paper to reveal your message!

The shortest verse in the Bible is John 11:35. It contains only two words: *Jesus wept*. Read it and find out why Jesus was sad.

Treasure #20

The Treasure of God's Gifts

I'M SINGING A SOLO IN CHURCH ON SUNDAY MORNING.

THAT'S GREAT, AMOS! I LOVE IT WHEN YOU SING. AND APPARENTLY EVERYONE ELSE DOES TOO, SINCE YOU GET LOTS OF APPLAUSE.

IT MUST FEEL GOOD TO HAVE PEOPLE APPLAUD YOU.

YEAH, BUT IT FEELS BETTER KNOWING THEY'RE REALLY APPLAUDING GOD.

1 PETER 4:10

Maybe you are someone who is very aware of how talented you are—someone who is good at sports or who can dance or draw or sing or does well in school. If so, thank God for your talents because all gifts come from God.

But what if you don't think you have any talents at all? Well, think again! God has gifted all of us with important talents that are perfectly suited to us and the plan He has for us. Spend time praying and talking with your parents to help you uncover your God-given gifts.

We are each unique with a special purpose designed by our Heavenly Father.

The important thing to remember is: Find your talents and use them in the way God intended, to help others.

God has given each of you a gift from his great variety of spiritual gifts. Use them well to serve one another.

What's Different?

CON LIKES TO DRAW.
HE'S DRAWN SIX PICTURES OF NIM.
WHICH TWO ARE THE SAME?
ONCE YOU KNOW, COLOR THEM ALL!

SILLY JOKE TIME:

Now It's Your Turn. How to Draw Con.

Con likes to draw Nim, and now you can learn to draw Con.

Just follow the instructions below:

STEP 1: USING A PENCIL,
DRAW THREE CIRCLES.

STEP 2:
DRAW TWO SQUARES FOR LEGS
AND TWO OVALS FOR FEET. ADD
EARS, EYES, NOSE, AND MOUTH.

STEP 3: ADD TAIL AND ARM. ERASE
LINES WHERE CIRCLES TOUCH.

STEP 4: USE A FELT TIP PEN TO
TRACE. ERASE PENCIL MARKS.

How do you fix a broken tomato?
With tomato paste!

Treasure #21

The Treasure of Hope

ONE OF GOD'S GREATEST TREASURES IS A SINGLE WORD...

Prof. Con

HOPE!!!

HOPE IS THE FUEL THAT PROPELS US TO DO GOD'S WORK ON EARTH.

AND YOU CAN TAKE THAT TREASURE TO THE BANK!

Prof. Con

90

ROMANS 5:5

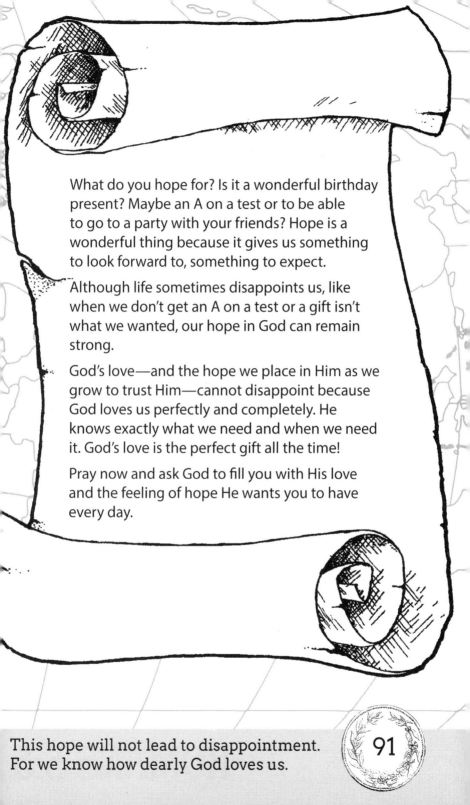

What do you hope for? Is it a wonderful birthday present? Maybe an A on a test or to be able to go to a party with your friends? Hope is a wonderful thing because it gives us something to look forward to, something to expect.

Although life sometimes disappoints us, like when we don't get an A on a test or a gift isn't what we wanted, our hope in God can remain strong.

God's love—and the hope we place in Him as we grow to trust Him—cannot disappoint because God loves us perfectly and completely. He knows exactly what we need and when we need it. God's love is the perfect gift all the time!

Pray now and ask God to fill you with His love and the feeling of hope He wants you to have every day.

This hope will not lead to disappointment.
For we know how dearly God loves us.

Hope You Can Finish This Word Search

```
F O H H M A T I W M F E E R A S Y B X U
A O F D W A N Q S Z L Q R R T R I E L P
H A C O B X W S H G H B Y F F J L L V W
U C C O R S T A D W V B R O L Q D I G M
G X V H I T V W O X T F X P M J A E X G
L P H M I R U H T P L C L O I V A F A R
R A N L X E E N N L T R E L I A N C E M
F G J X F N V L E U W I S Z W P W U W D
A D C A P H I E D J G O M Q N C Y S I U
I I D S R J G Y M B U C H I L G Z K S I
T E M U O T W H B E N W I S S H Q K H Y
H Z R L M J L K W Q N X A Y Y M V L U Y
M D A J I G H Q X V D T G T F G X N Y O
F Y J B S W H H M O T N X B Y U J G U R
O C L U E H I V A R I L R Y P R B N D Q
N W F S E K K Y P A J P N B T D I Q N E
H O P E N D D Y B D E S I R E A L E F V
J U V A F J G H U W W Y N Y R X I V Z A
C O N F I D E N C E W I B D C P M M R S
P B R I G H T N E S S N U N R H C B Y K
```

ACHIEVEMENT	BELIEF	BRIGHTNESS
CONFIDENCE	DESIRE	FAITH
FORTUNE	HOPE	OPTIMISM
PROMISE	RELIANCE	WISH

92

ROMANS 5:5

DIY: A Hope Journal

What You'll Need:

notebook (any size)	markers
pen or pencil	stickers
glue or tape	scissors
your Bible	craft or wrapping paper

First, make your book cover. Lay your sheet of craft paper or wrapping paper face down on a table. Place your book in the middle of your paper. Use a ruler to determine the size your cover needs to be, add 1 inch and trim your paper to that size. Fold the paper up against the top edge of your book and crease. Repeat for the bottom. Finish off the top and bottom edge by folding along the crease. This edge will be inside the paper, but outside the cover of your book.

With your book to the right of center, find where the front and back flaps will be. These should be around 1-2 inches wide and will tuck into your book. Trim away any excess paper and fold over front and back cover.

Attach the cover by folding the flaps over the existing cover. Tape or glue into place. Decorate your Hope Journal any way you want with markers, stickers, etc.

Now for the fun! Write your hopes and dreams inside the journal!

Abby's Tips for Journaling!

- Writing in your Hope Journal at the same time each day will help you establish the habit of journaling.
- Don't worry about what you say or draw—this is just for you! It is up to you whether or not you share your journal with anyone.
- Express yourself! Draw, color, or paint to make any picture you like.
- Try to find Bible promises and verses to help you. Write these in your Hope Journal to remind you of the hope we have in Jesus.

...because he has given us the Holy Spirit to fill our hearts with his love.

Treasure #22
The Treasure of the Holy Spirit

ROMANS 5:5

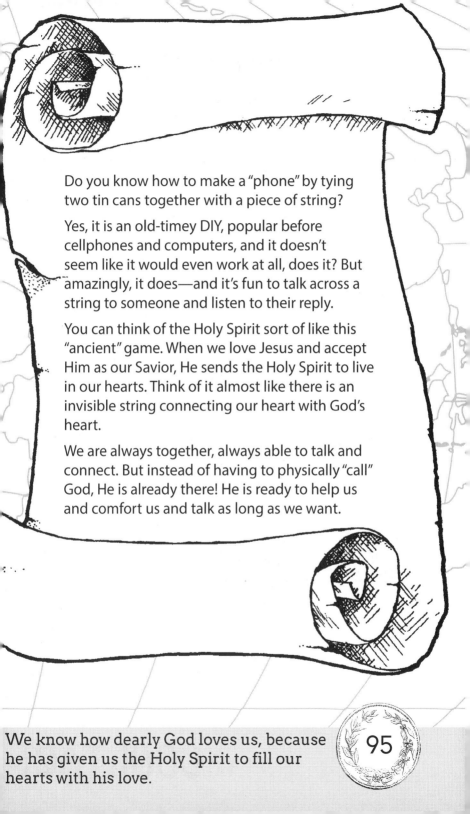

Do you know how to make a "phone" by tying two tin cans together with a piece of string?

Yes, it is an old-timey DIY, popular before cellphones and computers, and it doesn't seem like it would even work at all, does it? But amazingly, it does—and it's fun to talk across a string to someone and listen to their reply.

You can think of the Holy Spirit sort of like this "ancient" game. When we love Jesus and accept Him as our Savior, He sends the Holy Spirit to live in our hearts. Think of it almost like there is an invisible string connecting our heart with God's heart.

We are always together, always able to talk and connect. But instead of having to physically "call" God, He is already there! He is ready to help us and comfort us and talk as long as we want.

We know how dearly God loves us, because he has given us the Holy Spirit to fill our hearts with his love.

95

Help Amos Connect with Jerry

COOL FACT:

DIY: Flying Balloon Experiment

Help Professor Amos conduct a science experiment. Read and follow the instructions below. Be sure to ask a parent's permission first, and conduct this experiment outside. If you want, ask a friend to be your "assistant."

What You'll Need:

balloon
small empty water bottle
2 tablespoons baking soda
1/2 cup vinegar
drinking straw

10-foot piece of string
permanent marker
tape
scissors
pencil & paper

Here's How:

First, use the scissors to cut the straw in half. Next, thread the string through one piece of the straw. Use the tape to attach the string to an object, like a wall or window. Attach the other end of the string to another object that is several feet away. You could also tie the string to a tree or post, if desired.

Draw a face or design on your balloon using the permanent marker, if desired. Use the scissors to carefully cut the other part of the straw open and use it as a funnel to put the baking soda into the balloon. Hold the end of the balloon up so the baking soda won't fall out.

Now add 1/2 cup of vinegar to the empty water bottle. Carefully cover the water bottle opening with the opening of the balloon, and allow the baking soda to fall into the water bottle. Watch what happens! Use your paper and pencil to record your experiment, and make notes about the chemical reaction.

After the balloon inflates, pinch and twist the end of the balloon closed and remove it from the water bottle. Without tying the end of the balloon closed, tape the balloon to the piece of straw on the string. Now release the balloon and watch it fly across the string!

'he Holy Spirit is sometimes called the
Ioly Ghost, but we don't have to be afraid
f Him!

Treasure #23

The Treasure of Truth

THE BIBLE IS FULL OF PROMISES ABOUT TRUTH.

JOHN 8:32 SAYS "THE TRUTH SHALL SET YOU FREE."

IN JOHN 14:6, JESUS CALLS HIMSELF "THE TRUTH."

IN PSALMS, DAVID ASKS GOD TO "GUIDE ME IN YOUR TRUTH AND TEACH ME."

AND PROVERBS SAYS "EVERY WORD OF GOD IS FLAWLESS."

SO NO MATTER WHAT, YOU CAN ALWAYS TRUST WHAT GOD SAYS.

2 SAMUEL 7:28

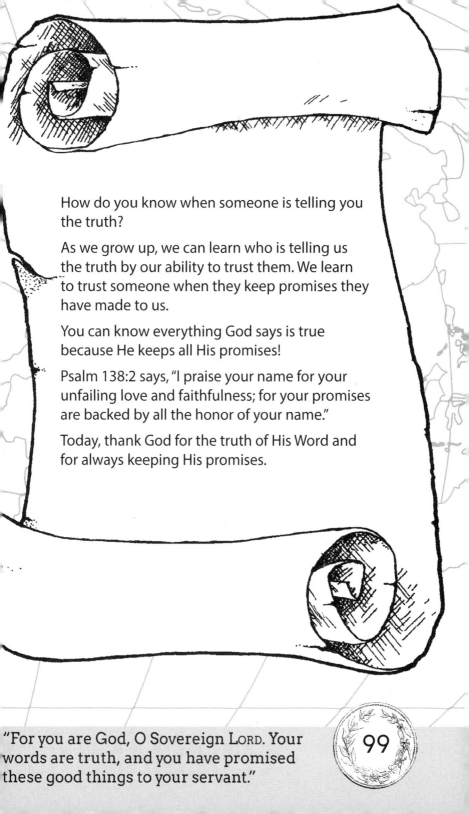

How do you know when someone is telling you the truth?

As we grow up, we can learn who is telling us the truth by our ability to trust them. We learn to trust someone when they keep promises they have made to us.

You can know everything God says is true because He keeps all His promises!

Psalm 138:2 says, "I praise your name for your unfailing love and faithfulness; for your promises are backed by all the honor of your name."

Today, thank God for the truth of His Word and for always keeping His promises.

"For you are God, O Sovereign LORD. Your words are truth, and you have promised these good things to your servant."

Wear the Belt of Truth Like Con

100

EPHESIANS 6:14

And That's the Truth!

Circle whether the statements below are true or false. Have your parents check your answers!

1. Penguins live in the deserts of Bora Bora.

True   False

2. Jesus was born in Bethlehem.

True   False

3. Genesis is the first book of the Bible.

True   False

4. Libraries are where you buy groceries and shoes.

True   False

5. It took God a month to create the earth.

True   False

6. Jesus is the Way, the Truth, and the Life.

True   False

7. Your hair is made of rubber and grease.

True   False

Stand your ground, putting on the belt of truth and the body armor of God's righteousness.

Treasure #24

Jesus Is Our Ultimate Treasure

WHAT'S UP, AMOS? WHY AREN'T YOU DRESSED FOR EXPLORING?

WE SAID WE WERE GOING TO LOOK FOR HIDDEN TREASURE.

I KNOW.

BUT I GAVE IT A LOT OF THOUGHT AND I REALIZED SOMETHING.

I'VE ALREADY FOUND MY TREASURE!

102

1 JOHN 4:10

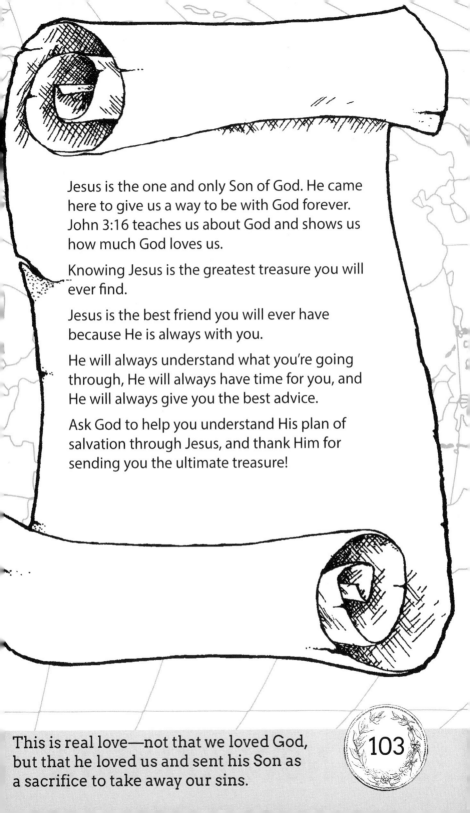

Jesus is the one and only Son of God. He came here to give us a way to be with God forever. John 3:16 teaches us about God and shows us how much God loves us.

Knowing Jesus is the greatest treasure you will ever find.

Jesus is the best friend you will ever have because He is always with you.

He will always understand what you're going through, He will always have time for you, and He will always give you the best advice.

Ask God to help you understand His plan of salvation through Jesus, and thank Him for sending you the ultimate treasure!

This is real love—not that we loved God, but that he loved us and sent his Son as a sacrifice to take away our sins.

Ultimate Treasure Word Search

```
K C N Q W T Q P R H A P U H B E E
U A L W A Y S S L S R B L V N B V
J Z R E F J X Y O J Q U T L C O E
Z L S A L V A T I O N Z I X Z J R
F F O R E V E R H U C Y M Y G F L
U S B M I M K X G H R R A N A C A
W T I F W X C Y A F X Z T P V Y S
W R V V U M C K Z C V W E R R E T
H E R H P D E V O T I O N K C V I
H A R X F K R P D S D G Z Q K E N
U S L Z M O E Y F W L L J H Q R G
U U M W H X W F L F E O I W N M C
Z R D V D B A Q M E I R P W E O E
B E H Q L L R H H I K Y S M O R T
F A B K W Y D C Z Z K H Y S Z E E
H H W M R L T Q T E F T Y P E Q R
V D A A Z X W N J L Q K V F L U N
J P B L R D I V I N E V S T A R A
A Z L A O D S M Z K D K B Y D I L
O P A M H Q C C I J B Y D D W T U
```

ALWAYS
AWARD
DEVOTION
DIVINE
ETERNAL
EVERLASTING
EVERMORE
FOREVER
GLORY
HALO
REWARD
SALVATION
STAR
TREASURE
ULTIMATE

Memorize It: John 3:16

John 3:16 is one of the most important verses in the Bible because it sums up what our faith is all about:

"For this is how God loved the world: He gave his one and only Son, so that everyone who believes in him will not perish but have eternal life."

104

NOW YOU KNOW...

Collect These Treasured Verses

Now that you know that Jesus is your Ultimate Treasure, look up these "Treasured Verses" in the Bible, write them on paper or index cards, and keep them near you all the time.

Luke 6:37

John 14:6

2 Peter 1:1

Matthew 16:23

Matthew 22:36–40

Matthew 6:33

Luke 11:9

Diamonds and gold are not as precious as our Lord, Jesus Christ!

Color Abby

DEAR DIARY-TO-GOD...
THANK YOU FOR ALL OF OUR
NEW FRIENDS! LOVE, ABBY

Color Amos

Color Jerry

Puzzle
Solutions

Treasure #1
Solutions

Let's Begin
THIS IS THE DAY THE LORD HAS MADE

Differences
Nim is smiling in one but not in the other.
Con's walking stick has a curled top in the second picture.
Nim's water bottle is not there in the second picture.
Con is wearing shoes in the first picture.
Nim's tail is up in the first picture.

Treasure #2
Solutions

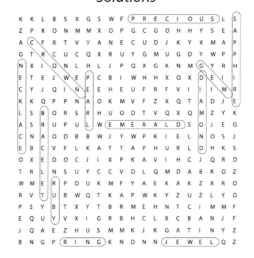

Treasure #4
Solutions

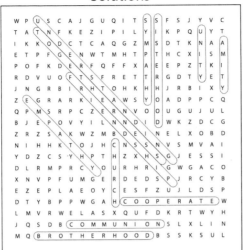

Treasure #5
Solutions

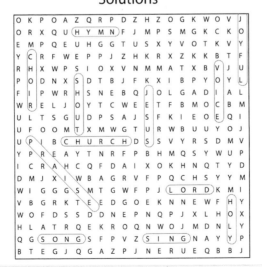

Treasure #8
Solutions

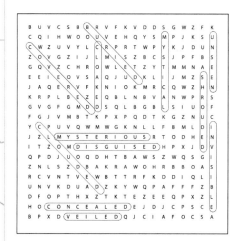

How did the dolphin trainer praise God?

By using his special porpoise!

Treasure #9
Solutions

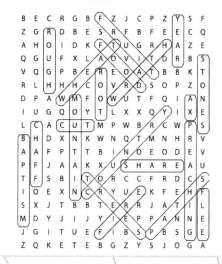

Treasure #10
Solutions

POLICE OFFICER
FIREFIGHTER
FIRE EXTINGUISHER
PASTOR
PARENT
FRIEND

Treasure #11
Solutions

WISDOM

Treasure #12
Solutions

IT'S A CROSS!

Treasure #13
Solutions

Treasure #14
Solutions

WHAT ARE YOU LOOKING HERE FOR?

YOU CREATED YOUR OWN SOLUTION!

Treasure #15
Solutions

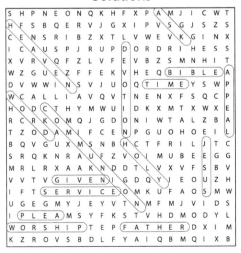

Treasure #16
Solutions

NICE JOB ON DRAWING YOUR HOUSE!

Treasure #17
Solutions

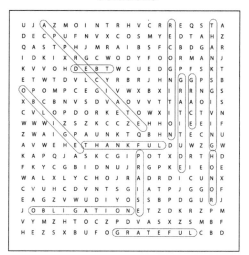

Treasure #18
Solution

What's the easiest way to get to heaven?

TURN RIGHT AND GO STRAIGHT!

Treasure #19
Solutions

FINDING THE RIGHT WORD:

LOVE
HAPPY
CARING
HOLY
SMART
LIFE

Treasure #20
Solutions

THE SECOND ONE AND THE SIXTH ONE ARE THE SAME!

NICE DRAWING THERE, PARTNER!

Treasure #21
Solutions

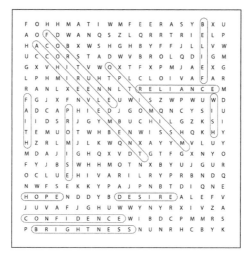

Treasure #22
Solutions

WASN'T THAT FLYING BALLOON COOL?

Treasure #23
Solutions

1. FALSE
2. TRUE
3. TRUE
4. FALSE
5. FALSE
6. TRUE
7. FALSE

Treasure #24
Solutions

```
K C N Q W T Q P R H A P U H B E E
U A L W A Y S S L S R B L V N B V
J Z R E F J X Y O J Q U T L C O E
Z L S A L V A T I O N Z I X Z J R
F F O R E V E R H U C Y M Y G F L
U S B M I M K X G H R R A N A C A
W T I F W X C Y A F X Z T P V Y S
W R V V U M C K Z C V W E R R E T
H E R H P D E V O T I O N K C V I
H A R X F K R P D S D G Z Q K E N
U S L Z M O E Y F W L L J H Q R G
U U M W H X W F L F E O I W N M C
Z R D V D B A Q M E I R P W E O E
B E H Q L L R H H I K Y S M O R T
F A B K W Y D C Z Z K H Y S Z E E
H H W M R L T Q T E F T Y P E Q R
V D A A Z X W N J L Q K V F L U N
J P B L R D I V I N E V S T A R A
A Z L A O D S M Z K D K B Y D I L
O P A M H Q C C I J B Y D D W T U
```

122

Get More Prayer Pups Fun!

Enjoy more comics and more fun at the *Prayer Pups* website!

PrayerPups.com

What We Believe

We believe the Bible is the eternal, infallible, authoritative Word of God.

We believe in the absolute deity of Jesus Christ. We believe He was born of a virgin, walked a sinless life, died on the cross for our sins, was resurrected in the flesh, ascended to heaven to be at the right hand of the Father, and in His future return.

We believe there is only one God, forever existent in three persons: the Father, the Son, and the Holy Spirit.

We believe people can receive forgiveness of sins and eternal life only through Jesus Christ.

We believe the meaning of life is to pursue a closer relationship with God through the Word of Jesus Christ.

We will never draw Jesus or any other biblical person as a cartoon character, because we believe doing so offers children the possibility of believing that these are make-believe characters as they grow older. Jesus is real, and should never be portrayed as a make-believe or comic character.

Jeffrey Smith & Sebrina Zerkus Smith

Acknowledgments

We would like to gratefully acknowledge the support of all of those who helped make this book possible.

At BroadStreet Publishing, David Sluka, Bill Watkins, Michelle Winger, and the rest of the team.

At WTA Group, our agent, Brian Mitchell.

We would also like to thank Matt and Amy Miller, Kevin McCallon, Maury and Nan Gill, Bo and Camille Zerkus, Sandy and Jerry Johnson, and all that have read and enjoyed *Prayer Pups* comics and *The Good Newz Children's Church Bulletins* since 2008.

And to all the real Prayer Pups we've known and loved: Bubu, Newton, Lenny, Casey, Nemo, Duke, Katie, Daisy, Jodi, Foxy, Dougal, Lynch, Max, Cocoa, Chloe, and Tootsie, thanks for making us laugh at your antics each and every day.

About the Author

Sebrina Zerkus Smith

Sebrina Zerkus Smith is a writer and blogger with a background in advertising and publications. Her clients include McDonald's, Madison Square Garden Event Productions, CBS, and Laurel Canyon Productions.

She has been a regular contributor for a number of media outlets including CNN.com, yahoo.com, wildoats.com, walmart.com, and others.

Since 2008, she has written devotions and created games and puzzles for *The Good Newz Children's Church Bulletins*, along with husband, Jeff. Together, they have helped children in fifteen countries learn the Word of God.

Sebrina recently published her book, *Cast Iron: All You Need to Know.*

About the Author

Jeffrey Smith

Jeff's background ranges from Hollywood to high tech. He began his career in advertising, writing, producing, and directing commercials for clients including McDonald's, Panasonic, and Sony. He moved his family to Los Angeles after being offered a producer role at Disney's promo department, where he created hundreds of trailers and TV spots.

He also co-created and produced the internationally-syndicated children's television show *Reel Planet*.

In 2007, Jeff decided to fulfill a lifelong dream and create a comic strip. It was at that time that he felt God pressing upon him to use the comic strip format to spread His Word. A few months later, *Prayer Pups* was born, and the comics are now read across America and in over 175 countries around the world.

Jeff and Sebrina live in Texas with their own little "Prayer Pugs," Newton and Lenny.

PRAYER PUPS

PrayerPups.com